FUN GROUP GAMES

FOR CHILDREN'S MINISTRY

Group

Loveland, Colorado

Group's R.E.A.L. Guarantee to you:

This Group resource incorporates our R.E.A.L. approach to ministry—one that encourages long-term retention and life transformation. It's ministry that's:

Relational
Because learner-to-learner interaction enhances learning and builds Christian friendships.

Experiential
Because what learners experience through discussion and action sticks with them up to 9 times longer than what they simply hear or read.

Applicable
Because the aim of Christian education is to equip learners to be both hearers and doers of God's Word.

Learner-based
Because learners understand and retain more when the learning process takes into consideration how they learn best.

FUN GROUP GAMES FOR CHILDREN'S MINISTRY

Copyright © 1990 and 2003 by Group Publishing, Inc.

Visit our Web site: **www.grouppublishing.com**

Credits
Editors: Lee Sparks and Mikal Keefer
Cover Art Director/Designer: Bambi Eitel
Art Director: Kari K. Monson
Print Production Artist: Joyce Douglas
Illustrator: Roc Goudreau

Library of Congress Cataloging-in-Publication Data
Fun group games for children's ministry.
    p.   cm.
    ISBN 0-7644-2526-9 (pbk. : alk. paper)
    1. Games in Christian education. 2. Church work with children. 3. Bible games and puzzles. I. Group
    Publishing
BV1536.3.F85 2003
268'.432—dc21   2002155782
                                             CIP

10 9 8 7 6 5 4 3 2 1   12 11 10 09 08 07 06 05 04 03
Printed in the United States of America.

CONTRIBUTORS

Karen Ball

Sandi Black

Jody Brolsma

Brian Cress

Carol Davant

Cindy Hansen

Margaret Hinchey

Delores Johnson

Janel Kauffman

Dawn Korth

Paul Lippard

Matt Lockhart

Amy Nappa

Jolene Roehlkepartain

Louisa Rogers

Linda Snyder

Norman Stolpe

Dave Thornton

Terry Vermillion

Brett Younger

Carol Younger

Chris Yount

CONTENTS

TEAMWORK BUILDERS

GAMES WITH A MESSAGE

BIBLE-LEARNING GAMES

ENERGY BURNERS

GROUP FUN

RELAYS

iNTRODUCTiON

Children love to play. And many child-development experts claim that children need to play more often these days. In our culture of the "hurried child" in which many forces are accused of pushing a child to grow up faster than he or she should, perhaps the ministry of play is one of the more valuable ministries of the church. And adults, if they're honest with themselves, will probably admit a degree of jealousy that children get to play more often than adults do.

In *Fun Group Games for Children's Ministry*, you'll find 100 active, creative games. There are games for increasing Bible knowledge, building community, enhancing teamwork, getting acquainted, and simply burning excess energy. Handy topical and Bible-passage indexes will help you select games that connect with your Bible lessons and themes.

You'll find an "energy-level" index in the back of the book too. Use it to help you pick a game that matches how much you want your kids moving during your lesson. Next to each game, you'll find an "instant energy-level indicator":

means it's a sizzling, high energy game involving running, walking, or physical interaction;

means there's some large muscle groups used but little or no movement; and

means there's fun but no movement.

Fun is a child magnet. Adding these tested, surefire games to your lessons is not only great fun for your kids, but it's also an opportunity for you to reinforce Bible lessons and values.

Have fun with *Fun Group Games for Children's Ministry*!

GETTING-TO-KNOW-YOU GAMES

BACKWARD AUTOGRAPHS
Psalm 33:14-15
God knows us

This is a fast-paced mixer or get-acquainted game.

You'll need a pencil and a piece of paper for each child.

Give children exactly three minutes (or more if it's a large group) to exchange autographs with as many others as they can. But each child must write his or her name backward. At the end of the time, the child who has collected the most signatures—and can identify whose they are—is the winner.

Say: **Even when we watch people write, we may have trouble knowing who wrote what. But God knows us and everything about us.**

• **How does it feel knowing God knows all your secrets?**

• **How does it feel knowing God knows all about you—and loves you anyway?**

BOP ON THE HEAD
Matthew 5:46-47
Greet newcomers

This is a great way to help children get to know one another's names.

You'll need enough chairs for the number of children in the group, minus one. You'll also need a "bat." Use something soft, such as a foam pool noodle.

Have children sit in a circle on chairs. Give one child the bat, and send him or her to the center.

Have one seated child start the game by saying his or her name and the name of someone else in the group. The person in the center then tries to "bop" on the knee the second person named before that person says his or her name and another person's name.

Any person who's bopped before he or she can say the second name then goes in the center to take the bat. The child who was formerly in the center sits down and starts the cycle over again by saying his or her name and the name of another child.

Say: **Sometimes it's uncomfortable meeting new people, but that's how friendships begin.**

- **What keeps us from reaching out to new people?**
- **How does it feel when someone reaches out to welcome you?**
- **What will you do today to reach out to newcomers?**

DRAW YOUR NEIGHBOR
1 Corinthians 12:12
Diversity

This activity helps children get acquainted and have fun drawing.

You'll need slips of paper, a hat or basket, blank pieces of paper for drawing, and pencils. Different-color pencils or markers can be used if desired. You'll also need tape or thumbtacks.

Have each child write his or her name on a slip of paper. Gather all the names in a hat or basket. Ask children to each draw a name but not to look at the people whose names they've picked. They're to keep the names they picked a secret. After everyone picks a name, have each child draw a picture of the person whose name he or she picked, without letting anyone see. Allow about ten minutes for drawing. Instruct children to draw just the faces of the people they picked. When they've finished, have children place the drawings in the middle of the floor, face down.

When all the drawings are in, shuffle them for added suspense, and then tape or tack them to a wall. Have children guess who each drawing represents and who drew the picture.

Drawings can be left on the wall or taped together to form a group portrait.

Say: **God made us different, but we all still fit!**

• **What's one thing you admire about the person you drew?**

• **What's one thing you like about yourself?**

• **How do you feel knowing that each person in your group—including you—is a special, unique creation of God?**

FOUR CORNERS
1 Corinthians 12:12-27
Diversity

This active game helps kids learn new things about each other. As you stand in the middle of the room and call out the choices on page 14, point to a corner for each choice. Have each child move to the corner that best fits him or her. Ask children to talk with the rest of the children in that corner about why they chose that corner. If time allows, call on someone from each corner to share what attracted kids to that corner.

The following are some sample categories.

My favorite food is

• hamburgers (point to corner #1).

- pizza (point to corner #2).
- steak (point to corner #3).
- seafood (point to corner #4).

My favorite vacation is

- going to Disneyland (point to corner #1).
- skiing (point to corner #2).
- swimming at the beach (point to corner #3).
- visiting relatives (point to corner #4).

My favorite room in the house is

- the kitchen (point to corner #1).
- the family room (point to corner #2).
- my bedroom (point to corner #3).
- the bathroom (point to corner #4).

Other options: spectator sports, participatory sports, school subjects, games or TV shows. Pick things that interest your group.

Say: **There's a lot of variety in our group—and that's good!**

- **Why do you think God made us so we're different?**
- **Why is it important to accept and love people who are different from us?**
- **What's one way in which God has made you a special, unique person?**

FRIEND ACROSTIC
1 Samuel 2:2-3
God knows us

This noncompetitive activity helps children reveal facts about themselves.

For each child, you'll need a pencil and a piece of paper with a word or phrase spelled out vertically down the left margin. You can use the name of your group, a greeting, or any appropriate word or phrase that has fewer total letters than the number of participants.

Have each child go to other children and get them each to write something about themselves that starts with a letter in the vertical word or phrase. Here's an example:

Has three sisters

Elephants—She collects them.

Loves music

Long hair

Ordinarily skips breakfast

The first person who gets his or her acrostic completely filled out and can match each fact with the appropriate child is the winner.

Say: **God knows us. Let's get to know each other!**

• **What's something you discovered about someone that surprised you?**

• **What's something you told another person that you haven't shared before?**

• **How does it feel knowing that God knows everything about you?**

GREAT IMPRESSIONS
John 13:34-35
Growing in Jesus

This nonthreatening activity helps children associate themselves with things around them.

You'll need enough clay, Silly Putty, or Play-Doh for each person to have a small piece.

Give each child a piece of clay, Silly Putty, or Play-Doh. Then ask children each to leave the room and make an impression on the clay of something in the church. For example, the tread from the bottom of the pastor's shoe, the words on the cover of a Bible, or a heating vent. Then have children take turns showing their impressions to the group while others guess what they are. After each correct guess, have the child who made that impression explain why he or she chose that item.

Say: **When we know, love, and follow Jesus, it leaves an impression on us.**

• **In what ways does your life show that you've been with Jesus?**

• **How would you like to see Jesus change you and help you grow even more?**

LIST GAME
Romans 12:16
Friendship

This activity helps children discover things they have in common.

You'll need a large piece of poster board and markers. For each child, you'll need a pencil and a piece of paper numbered from one to ten.

Use the poster board and markers to create a numbered list of ten things that children have in common. Place the list where everyone can see it. Give each child a pencil and piece of paper numbered from one to ten. On "go," have the children each find someone who fits the description of one of the numbered items. Have the "discovered" child sign the other child's paper next to the appropriate number. If your group is large, make a rule that there can be no repeats. The list might read:

1. Someone who uses the same color toothbrush as you do.
2. Someone who has the same last digit in his or her phone number as you do.
3. Someone who has the same shoe size as you do.
4. Someone who was born in the same state as you were.
5. Someone who has the same number of brothers and sisters as you do.
6. Someone who was born in the same month as you were.
7. Someone whose family has the same kind of car as your family does.
8. Someone who had the same thing for breakfast as you did.
9. Someone who has the same favorite food as you do.
10. Someone who goes to the same dentist as you do.

Say: **We have lots in common—more than we think!**

• **How do you feel when you discover you have something in common with another person?**

• **What do you think it takes to live in harmony with others?**

• **In what ways is Jesus a friend of yours?**

MAP YOUR LiFE
Genesis 12:1-4
Abraham/Following God

This is a nonthreatening activity that helps children share where they were born, where they would like to visit, and where they would *not* like to visit.

You'll need a big map of North America or, better yet, the world. You'll also need a few markers.

Post the map on the wall in your meeting room. Have children mark the following three spots with their initials:

- where they were born,
- one place they want to visit, and
- one place they hope not to visit (a jungle, desert, or icy sea, for instance).

After each child has marked his or her three spots, point to each spot and have the child whose initials are there tell why he or she chose that place.

Say: **Abraham didn't pick where he would move; he followed God's directions to wherever God wanted to take him.**

- **Is following God a good idea? Why or why not?**
- **How would you feel if God led you to a place you didn't want to go?**
- **What's something you've done because you were following God?**

MEETIN' MEETINGS
John 15:11-13
Friendship

This fast-paced game encourages kids to share about themselves. For each team you'll need a lightweight object that can be tossed onto laps, such as a Nerf ball or handkerchief.

Form teams of three or four. Give each team a Nerf ball, handkerchief, or any lightweight object that can be tossed onto laps. Have the person with the longest shoelaces start.

The first player tosses the object onto a teammate's lap while everyone claps slowly in unison. As the object is tossed, he or she calls out one of four categories:

- family,
- friends,
- room, or
- school.

The receiver must catch the object, then call out an object or person in his or her life that fits that category. For example, if "friends" is called out, the receiver might say, "John." The receiver must call out an answer within two claps. Then it's his or her turn to toss the object. If a receiver fails, possession returns to the player who tossed the object.

Allow three to five minutes. Then have each team's players say their own names. Then have their teammates tell all they learned about each child. For example, "Katie has a desk in her room." Give each piece of information 1 point.

After all children have been introduced, the team with the most points wins.

Say: **It's easier to love people if we know them!**

- **What's something new you learned about a friend today?**
- **What's something you'd like others to know about you?**
- **What will you do to help form friendships?**

NAME GAME
Genesis 35:10
Friendship

All you need is an old sock filled with cotton and tied closed to help children learn each other's names.

Have children sit in a circle. Designate one person to be "It." He or she sits in the middle, armed with the cotton-filled sock. One child starts by saying someone else's name in the circle. The child named must then name another child in the circle before getting walloped with the flying sock.

When a child gets hit with the sock, he or she becomes the new "It." The former "It" joins the circle and starts a new round by calling out a name. If "It" throws the sock after the child has said a name, "It" stays in the middle.

Say: **In the Bible, God sometimes changes the names of people to show a change in character. Today we'll work on learning names!**

• **Some names have special meanings. If you know, share what your name means. What do you wish it meant?**

• **If you could have any name you wanted, other than the name you have, what would you choose? Why?**

• **In what ways are you a friend who's worth remembering? What could you do to be an even better friend?**

PEOPLE PLACE MATS

Luke 19:1-9
Zacchaeus/Sharing ourselves

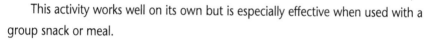

This activity works well on its own but is especially effective when used with a group snack or meal.

For each child, you'll need a marker and an inexpensive white paper place mat.

Place the markers and place mats around on tables. As children come in, have each one sit in front of a place mat. Ask the kids to divide their place mats into four sections with the markers. Have children number the corners and use their best creative ability to describe the following things:

Square 1—Draw a symbol that represents your family when they're together.

Square 2—Draw a symbol of what you want to be when you're older.

Square 3—Draw a picture of what you enjoy most with your friends.

Square 4—Draw a picture of your favorite Christmas or other holiday.

Have children each share their drawings with four children around them or with the whole group, depending on the size of the group.

Say: **Being with Jesus brought about change in Zacchaeus. And Jesus knew Zacchaeus!**

• **What do you think Zacchaeus told Jesus about himself during the meal they shared?**

• **What would you like to tell Jesus about yourself? Why?**

PUZZLE PARTNERS
Proverbs 13:7
Listening

This get-acquainted activity can be used to divide kids into pairs or smaller groups.

You'll need pictures cut from magazines, and if you wish, copies of the discussion-starters below.

Cut out magazine pictures that show people involved in various activities. Cut each picture into two or more pieces.

Give each child a piece of a picture. Have children mill around and find out who has other pieces of their pictures. Then have each pair or small group with the same picture sit together, assemble the picture, and talk together. Some discussion-starters:

• How are you like someone in the picture?

• If you were in the scene pictured, what would you be doing? saying?

• What incident in your life does the picture remind you of?

• If a member of your family saw you doing what's pictured, what would he or she say?

• Where would you rather be—in the picture or in math class? Why?

For a variation on the game, have pairs or small groups each create a caption for their picture. Then have the large group choose the most creative caption as the winner. Or have pairs or small groups create skits based on their pictures to perform for everyone else.

Say: **When we meet people, we don't usually have the whole picture. It takes asking questions and listening to get to know others.**

• **How long do you think it takes to really get to know someone?**

• **What are two things you can do to get to know others better?**

READ AND MATCH

Genesis 2:18-24
Adam

Before the meeting, collect subscription cards from various magazines. You'll need two cards from each magazine. Scramble the cards.

When children arrive, give each child one card. Have each child search for another child who has a card from the same magazine without saying the name of the magazine. Instead, children must ask yes-or-no questions about the magazine, such as "Does your magazine deal with animals?" or "Is your magazine for adults?"

When children find their partners, have pairs choose which of the two cards grabs their attention more. Then have the child who's holding that card say what he or she enjoys reading and why. Then have the partner do the same.

Say: **Adam had met lots of animals, but he wanted to meet someone like himself—a person. We like to be with people who are like us.**

• **If you could pick someone to meet for the first time, who would you pick, and why?**

• **Who's a friend of yours who you remember meeting for the first time? What did you think of that person then?**

• **People are important! What will you do today to show that people matter to you?**

WHICH ARE YOU LIKE?

Isaiah 44:24
God knows you

This activity helps children develop a sense of themselves and others.

Before the meeting, create a series of pairs of related but contrasting items, such as "breakfast/dinner" or "winter/summer." Some examples:

a couch or a rocking chair	a TV show or a book
green or yellow	plastic or wood
water or earth	an attic or a basement
pizza or ice cream	a folk song or a popular hit
a freeway or a country road	an onion or an apple
a bath or a shower	north or south
Saturday or Wednesday	a candle or a flashlight
corduroy or denim	a kite or a Frisbee

Have children mingle in a large, open space. Then call out one pair of items, using the question "Are you more like____ or____?" Have children go to one side of the room if they feel like one item or the other side of the room if they feel like the opposite item. No in-betweeners allowed!

Randomly select children from each side of the room. Ask each child to explain why he or she feels more like one item than the other. After three or four kids have contributed, have the group return to the middle of the room to start on the next pair of items. Repeat the game as long as you wish.

Say: **God formed you in your mother's womb. God knows you—every bit of you, everything *about* you. And he wants what's best for you because he loves you.**

- **Who is the person you think knows you best? Why?**
- **How does it feel knowing that God knows you so well? Why?**

TEAMWORK BUILDERS

BLINDFOLD ART

2 Corinthians 3:17-18

Reflecting God's glory

Trios of kids will work together in this drawing game. It will take ten to thirty minutes, depending on the number of drawings you choose to do.

You'll need a blindfold for each trio. Each trio will need a pencil, a pad of paper, and slips of paper with words for players to illustrate.

Here's how you play: You'll have kids form trios, then have one member of each trio come up to see you. That child will be the "illustrator" in his or her trio. You'll give that child a slip of paper with a word on it that the child will illustrate while blindfolded.

Show each illustrator a word from your stack of words, then send illustrators back to their trios to be blindfolded. Give illustrators thirty to forty-five seconds to illustrate their words as their partners watch. The other members of each illustrator's trio will guess what's being illustrated.

Rules:

1. No spelling out words!

2. Illustrators can't speak.

Some suggestions for words to use: socks, garden, pineapple, cactus, ski, basketball, mother, tornado, scissors, caterpillar, kick, camel, toenail, radio, mountain goat, diaper, notebook, smoke, yawn, zebra, cook, wheelchair, bus, puzzle, stop, clown, principal, pastor, cry, pretzel, radio, beach, window, shade, pay telephone, string bean, oatmeal cookie, moustache, spare tire, hubcap, school crossing zone, meatloaf, rubber band, sunset, sunrise.

Say: **It's tough to reflect the glory of a sunrise when you can't see what you're drawing! Still, a little bit of that beauty came through on our drawings.**

• **In what ways does the glory of God shine through in your life?**

• **In what ways would you like God's glory to shine through even more?**

BEANBAG VOLLEYBALL
Ephesians 5:15-17
Priorities

For this variation of volleyball, you'll need a volleyball net, four to six beanbags, and a whistle. Put a piece of tape on one of the beanbags.

Divide your group into two teams, with one team on each side of the net. Give each team an equal number of beanbags. The more beanbags, the crazier the game.

At the sound of the whistle, have teams toss their beanbags over the net. No spiking! The opposing team will try to catch the tossed beanbags and throw them back over the net.

If a beanbag is caught, the team that catches it gets a point. If the team catches the beanbag with the piece of tape on it, *two* points are scored. If a beanbag falls to the floor, it's picked up and tossed over the net with no point scored.

Once one team has scored ten points, have children count off by threes. Swap the Threes on one team for the Twos on the other team. Do another countdown and swap when a team scores eighteen points. The game then continues until one side or the other scores twenty-one points.

No player can hold a beanbag more than three seconds or pass it more than once before the bag is tossed over the net.

Say: **It's easy to be overwhelmed by everything we need to do at school, home, and church. But what's the most important thing you can do?**

• **Describe the activities that fill you calendar. How many are there?**

How do you feel about them?

• **If you had to pick one activity that's the most important, what would you pick? Why?**

• **What do you think God wants as your top priority? Why? Is it your top priority?**

BURST A BUBBLE

Romans 15:5-6

Encourage others

This game gives kids a chance to burn energy and have fun.

You'll need two jars of bubble mixture. Buy these in grocery or discount stores, or make your own by mixing one part liquid Ivory soap with two parts water. Empty thread spools can be used as bubble-blowers. Bring bubble gum for prizes.

Have kids number off using "bubble" or "burst" instead of numbers. Then have all "bubbles" form one team and all "bursts" form another.

Give one person on each team a jar of bubble mixture. Have that person be the team's bubble-blower. Also, have one person on each team try to pop as many bubbles as he or she can. Have the other team members count the number of burst bubbles. On "go," have the bubble-blowers blow bubbles. Change bubble-blowers and bubble-poppers after one minute. Continue until each team member has played.

Ask the teams to add their total number of burst bubbles. Award two pieces of bubble gum to each winning team member. Give the other team members each one piece for a job well done.

Say: **It's easy to "burst someone's bubble" with a harsh word or criticism.**

• Why do we sometimes feel the need to burst another person's bubble?

• When is a time you had your bubble burst by criticism? How did you feel?

• What will you do to encourage one person today?

CRAB SOCCER
Hebrews 10:35-37
Perseverance

This game follows the basic rules of soccer, except kids play indoors. And it's less competitive since all players are "crabs." Even nonathletic kids enjoy this game, and everyone gets a good laugh.

You'll need a soccer ball. Set up goals like soccer, only smaller.

Form two teams and play soccer. But have all players walk and kick the ball like crabs—with their bellies in the air and walking on all fours. Encourage teams to "strategize" just like they would in soccer.

Say: **To play this game takes perseverance—you have to keep going even though you get tired. The Christian life can be like that sometimes.**

• What's a time you showed perseverance even though you thought you couldn't finish something? What was it?

• Tell about a time you did what God wanted you to do even though you were tired, angry, or discouraged. What happened?

• What will you think about to encourage yourself the next time you get tired or discouraged?

MELT THE iCE!
Ecclesiastes 4:9-10

Working together

This activity helps kids learn about sharing and working together. You'll need a supply of equal-sized ice cubes.

Form two teams. Have each team stand in a circle, facing inward. Give each team an ice cube. The goal is for each team to melt its ice cube as quickly as possible as the cube is passed around the circle. No one child can have the cube for more than ten seconds before passing it to the next person.

At your signal, have the child in each circle who has the shortest hair be first to pick up the ice cube you've placed on the floor in the middle of each circle. Then the cubes will be passed to the right. Cubes can be held, placed under arms, rubbed on arms, even put in mouths (Yuck! Don't let kids do this!); anything to melt the cube.

Say: **The goal was to melt the ice as quickly as possible. That took working together!**

• **If one person had held the cube tightly until the cube melted, how could the cold have hurt that person?**

• **Describe a time you worked in a team and enjoyed it. What happened?**

• **What do you think would help you be a better team player?**

HOLLY-JOLLY OBSTACLE COURSE

Luke 2:1-20

Christmas

This game can be used during Christmas season. It burns off lots of energy.

You'll need inflated inner tubes, straw or hay, scarves, hats, mittens, songbooks, tree branches, tinsel, ornaments, ice water, tubs, green hats, hammers, boards, nails, red hats, toys, bags, crowns, boxes of "jewels," housecoats, and towels.

Before the group arrives, set up the course for two teams in two separate lines.

Form two teams. Each team sends one person at a time through the series of activities. The object is to be the first team to get every team member through the course.

At each activity the child completes a task relating to Christmas:

• **Manger**—Put straw or hay in the middle of an inner tube and then sit in it.

• **Caroler**—Put on a scarf, hat, and mittens; pick up a songbook; and sing "Joy to the World!"

• **Christmas Tree**—Decorate a tree branch with an ornament and five pieces of tinsel.

• **Chilly Water**—Walk through a tub of ice water.

• **Elf**—Put on a green hat and hammer a nail into a board.

• **Santa**—Put on a red hat, put toys in a bag, and say, "Ho, ho, ho."

• **Wiseman**—Put on a crown, pick up a box of jewels, and say, "Follow that star!"

• **Shepherd**—Put on a housecoat, place a towel on your head, and look for your sheep.

Say: **It's easy to get so busy at Christmastime that we forget Jesus. Let's not do that this year!**

• **What's your favorite Christmastime activity?**

• **How does that activity remind you of Jesus' birth?**

• **What's something you can do this holiday season to make sure you remember Jesus?**

MACARONI MESSAGES
2 Timothy 3:16-17
The Bible

This word game can be used for individual, partner, or team competition.

You'll need approximately one box of dry alphabet macaroni for every four to six players.

Spill the macaroni on a table in front of the players where everyone can reach it. Then call out clues like the ones on page 29. Players grab for letters and spell out words in front of them. Pairs or teams can work together.

The first person, pair, or team to form a word earns a point, and the team with the most points after a set time wins.

Some clues: a circus animal, a name of a car, a kind of soap, a fighter uses, what a baby does, a day of the week, a subject stud__ of a department store, a sport, a cartoon character, an article of clothing, an ice cre_ flavor, a name of a big city, a vegetable, a fast-food restaurant.

Say: **The Bible "spells out" many ways to live and please God.**

• **What's something in the Bible you don't understand?**

• **In what ways does the Bible help you make good choices?**

MiTTEN MENACE

Romans 12:6-8

Skills and gifts

This game helps "equalize" the motor skills of kids so all can play comfortably.

For each team, you'll need a pair of mittens, a paper bag, some individually wrapped pieces of candy, and yarn.

Form two equal teams. Have each team form a circle. Give each team a pair of mittens and a paper bag with a piece of candy for each team member. Tie each paper bag shut with a piece of yarn.

On "go," have one child on each team put on the mittens and untie the bag. With the mittens still on, have the person pull out one piece of candy, unwrap it, and retie the yarn around the bag. Then have him or her pass the mittens and bag to the person on his or her left. Have teams continue until everyone has participated.

Variation: Instead of candy, use fortune cookies and have each person read his or her fortune aloud after eating the cookie.

Say: **We're all good at different things, and God can use what we have to offer to encourage and serve others.**

• **Who's someone who uses his or her gifts or skills to encourage you? In what way?**

• **What's a hobby or skill you have?**

• **How can God use that hobby or skill to help others?**

MUSICAL INSTRUMENTS
Psalm 150
Praise

Form groups of two to ten players. Have each group move into its own space (different rooms, if possible) and—without any props or materials—create a musical instrument complete with sound and movement. Give groups exactly five minutes. Then have each group perform its instrument. Re-form different groups and play again.

Say: **We can praise God with so many things, including our bodies!**

• **Why do you think praising God is important?**

• **What's your favorite way to praise God?**

ONE-HANDED ART
Galatians 5:12-13
Serving others

This noncompetitive activity for partners requires children to work together. You'll need art supplies such as modeling clay, construction paper, glue, string,

crayons, markers, and paint. A wide variety of materials is nice but not required.

Form pairs. Instruct partners to work together to create something using materials of their choice. But each partner can use only one hand. Right-handers must use their left hands, and left-handers must use their right hands. Both partners must contribute to the creation.

Say: **Sometimes we have to work together to accomplish a task or reach a goal. That's so much easier if we know how to serve each other!**

- **What "service job" do you think you would enjoy most?**
- **Who is someone who serves you?**
- **How can you serve someone who lives with you today?**

PEOPLE SCRAMBLE
Acts 2:36-37
Leadership

This game requires kids to think and act quickly to spell words.

You'll need markers, tape, and a few pieces of paper. Form two teams. Ask an adult volunteer to be the scribe for each team.

Tape a piece of paper with one letter of the alphabet on the front of each team-mate. For example, if you have five players on each team, use letters such as R, S, T, N, and A. Add letters if you have more players. Each child should get a different letter. Each team should get a different set of letters to encourage creativity. Be sure each team has a vowel or two.

On "go," have children scramble and rearrange themselves to spell as many nonoffensive words as they can think of using as many of the players as they wish. Have the scribe write the words formed by the players. For example, using the letters above, the kids could spell: at, tar, as, rat, star, tan, Stan, an, ran, and sat.

After five minutes, stop to see which team has created the most words.

Say: **Games like this go nowhere until someone steps into leadership and gets things organized.**

- **How do you feel when someone leads you?**
- **Describe a time you were a leader. What happened? How did you feel?**

PINGPONG BLOW
1 Kings 19:11-13
God's voice

Got any windbags in your group? Here's a game that'll blow off a lot of steam. You'll need several pingpong balls and some masking tape.

Form two teams. Have teams kneel on opposite sides of a large table. Put a line of masking tape down the middle of the table between the two teams.

Have all team members clasp their hands behind their backs. Have players try to blow pingpong balls across the table to fall off the table on the opponent's side.

Start with one pingpong ball, but gradually add more until you have about seven balls going at once. The team to get the most pingpong balls blown off the opponent's side within five minutes wins.

Say: **The team that was the most powerful and could blow hardest stood a good chance of winning this game. God is always most powerful, but sometimes he speaks and acts very softly. We have to listen!**

• **Describe a time you saw God's power at work.**

• **Describe a time you listened and God led you. How did he do it? How did you feel?**

• **What's a situation in which you would like God to lead you?**

PUZZLE TRADE
Ephesians 2:10
Life

This game is a fun teamwork-builder game for any number of small teams.

For each team, you'll need a large picture or poster, a plastic bag, and several pairs of scissors.

Form teams of three. Give each team a different picture or poster, and have teams cut their pictures apart to create jigsaw puzzles. Have teams keep their pictures a secret and make the puzzles as difficult as possible. Explain that they'll be exchanging puzzles with another team. No puzzle piece may be smaller than one square inch. You might also want to set a limit on the number of puzzle pieces. Give the teams a few minutes to create the puzzles, but don't rush them.

After teams have completed their puzzles, instruct them to each put the puzzle pieces in a plastic bag. Place all the puzzles in a pile. Have each team choose a runner.

On "go," have the runners dash to the pile, grab a puzzle that's not their team's, and take it back to their team to be assembled.

Say: **Does it sometimes feel like your life is a puzzle you're struggling to assemble? and you don't have all the pieces?**

• **Describe a "missing piece" of your puzzle. What's something you wish you knew?**

• **When you think about your future, do you feel confident or scared? Explain.**

PYRAMID RACES

Proverbs 16:18-19

Pride

No doubt you've seen or been in a human pyramid. But this game adds another dimension to human pyramids: They move.

Form teams of three. Designate a turn-around point about twenty feet away. Have two children from each team get down on their hands and knees side by side. Have the third child kneel on top of the two kneeling teammates. Be sure the child on top isn't too heavy for the kids below.

Ask teams to predict how long it will take them to crawl to the designated point and back without the top person falling off. Then let them try!

And safety first! Play this game in a place where falling won't create injuries.

Say: **This was harder than it looked, so for some of us pride literally came before a fall!**

• **Why do you think we tend to be so proud?**

• **Describe a time you were proud of your abilities and then fell flat. What happened? How did you feel?**

• **What will you do to remember to not be overly proud or proud of the wrong things?**

QUESTIONABLE FOOTBALL
Luke 1:5-20
Questioning God

This game is a good activity anytime, but especially so in the fall when football commands so much attention.

Form two teams. Each team huddles and chooses an object for their opponents to guess. The object doesn't need to be in the room. Line up the two teams facing each other, with several feet between them. Using masking tape, mark one-foot lines between the teams, to look somewhat like a football gridiron. Toss a coin to decide who "kicks off."

The player on the far right of the line begins by asking the player facing him or her a yes-or-no question about the object. A "yes" wins a "first down." The team keeps possession. The next teammate asks a question. A "no" causes a "turnover." Play continues using the rules below until one team scores a "touchdown."

• **First Down**—When the team takes one step forward to the next line after a "yes."

• **Forward Pass**—When a player makes a correct guess on the object before the team has crossed the goal line. This scores a touchdown.

• **Fumble**—When a player makes an incorrect guess on a forward pass. The entire team must return to the starting line.

• **Turnover**—When possession passes to the rival team after a "no."

• **Huddle**—Time out. Two per team allowed to plan strategy and questions to ask.

• **Touchdown**—Wins the game. Can be achieved through either a forward pass or a series of first downs. When the entire team crosses the goal line, the team must make a guess. If the team guesses correctly, it wins. If not, the entire team returns to the starting line.

Say: **Zechariah got in trouble when he questioned God—not because Zechariah had a question, but because he wasn't looking for information. He was expressing doubt. Honest questions don't anger God!**

• **How do you feel when you're asked questions? when you ask them?**

• **What's a question you would ask God if you had the chance?**

RACING DR. SEUSS

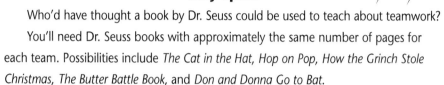

Philippians 4:6-7

Holy Spirit

Who'd have thought a book by Dr. Seuss could be used to teach about teamwork?

You'll need Dr. Seuss books with approximately the same number of pages for each team. Possibilities include *The Cat in the Hat, Hop on Pop, How the Grinch Stole Christmas, The Butter Battle Book,* and *Don and Donna Go to Bat.*

Form teams of four or five. Give each team a Dr. Seuss book. Have the children sit in a circle. Have each child read a page of the book aloud and act out an action on that page. If there are no verbs, have children imitate sounds, characters, or silly nouns on the page. Then have that child pass the book to the next child, who reads the next page and does the same thing.

Say: **When everyone is talking and moving at once, it's chaos, confusing, not peaceful!**

The Holy Spirit brings peace into our lives as we grow closer to God.

• **In what ways do you lack peace in your life?**

• **In what ways does knowing God help you feel peaceful?**

SNAKE

Mark 9:34-35

Servanthood

Have kids make a human snake, and have a lot of fun. You don't need any materials, just add kids.

Form at least two teams. Have the teams gather behind a starting line. The object is to make a human snake that stretches around the room, gym, or hallway; around a goal; and back to the starting line. The longer the course, the better.

On "go," the first child on each team lies on the ground with his or her hands on the starting line and feet stretched down-field. As soon as the first child is lying down, the second child runs and grabs the feet of the first child and lies down. As soon as the second child is lying down, the third child grabs the second child's feet and lies down, and so on.

When everyone in line is lying down as part of the snake, have the first person get

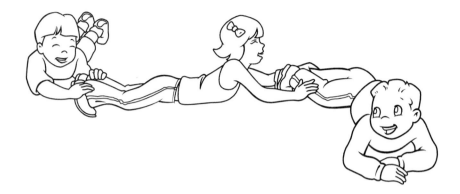

up, run to the end of the snake and hook on again. Then have children continue the action until the team completes the course.

It's best to have an adult at the head of each line to tell each child when he or she can run to the end of the snake.

Say: **In this activity, the first in line quickly found themselves last in line.**

• **When have you found yourself suddenly last? How did that feel?**

• **God insists that all who serve him be servants to others. Why do you think he does this?**

• **In what ways do you serve others?**

THE DAVID MYSTERIES

1 Samuel 25

Cooperation

Children love mysteries. Here's a game that lets kids be super sleuths as they explore the life of David.

You'll supply the questions and clues for this game. David had a celebrated encounter with Goliath, but many of his other relationships are largely unexplored by kids. You'll devise a game that helps children dig into David's past and gets kids to use their Bibles.

On a white board, place sections of Scripture that contain David's encounters with key characters. Then give children a clue from a specific encounter, and ask children to work in teams to deduce who's the mystery person for whom they're searching. For instance, you might include 1 Samuel 25 and give the clue "roasted grain."

This clue will lead children to identifying Abigail.

Among other encounters are Saul, Jonathan, and Mephibosheth.

Say: **Finding the mystery person was easier when we worked in teams.**

• **What do you like most about working in a team? What do you like least?**

• **What's hardest for you when it comes to cooperating with others?**

• **What would help you cooperate better with others?**

FEEDING ELIJAH

1 Kings 17:1-6
Elijah

You'll need a five-foot length of string and a box of uncooked elbow macaroni for each team.

Form teams of four to seven people. Ask members of each team to line up single file behind a starting line. Hand the first child on each team the string with a large knot tied in one end and the macaroni.

At your signal, the first person will string one piece of macaroni and run it to the other end of the string. As soon as the macaroni is snuggly at the other end of the string, the next person will string the second piece of macaroni. Kids will continue, rotating the task. The goal is for the teams to fill their strings with macaroni.

Say: **We brought food to the knot, like birds brought food to Elijah.**

• **How do you think Elijah felt having to rely on birds for food?**

• **Tell about a time you had to rely on someone else. What happened? How did you feel?**

SUPER SNIFFERS

Proverbs 3:5-6
Trust

This game's nothing to sneeze at!

You'll need a dozen spices, such as oregano, basil, thyme, chili powder, dill, garlic, and turmeric. Put ¼ teaspoon of each spice or herb into a separate small paper lunch bag. Number each bag, and tie it partially shut with a piece of yarn so that kids can smell what's inside but can't see what's inside.

Create a second, identical set of bags, and put a unique, random letter on each bag to identify it. Don't use sequential letters that make it easy to know in which order the bags were filled.

Form two teams. Give one team the numbered bags and the other team the bags identified by letters. Give teams two minutes to match up a letter with a number—they'll have to sniff out which bags contain identical spices.

At the end of the two minutes, see which team was best able to "sniff out" the truth!

Say: **One way to discover truth is to sniff it out in person. But what if your senses can't confirm the information? That's where trust comes in!**

- **What sorts of things help you trust others?**
- **Is God trustworthy? Why or why not?**
- **What can you do to show that you have trust in God?**

TEAM CROSSWORD

Hebrews 12:1-2

Perseverance/Patience

This is a large-scale team game that requires children to work well with one another to win.

For each team, you'll need fifty pieces of paper with a letter of the alphabet printed on each one. You'll also need a sheet of clues for each team.

Give each team these fifty letters:

6—E

5 each—A I O

3 each—R N T U

2 each—L M S Z

1 each—B C D F H K P W Y

Have each team create a giant crossword puzzle on the floor or ground, forming words from clues you give them. Some clues to use: where you spend most of your time, name of your favorite food, what you want for your birthday, something you read, a musical instrument, a kind of pet, a month of the year, a toy you once played with, your favorite color, something with stripes.

Score one point for each letter used. It's not absolutely necessary for words to intersect, but each word that successfully intersects another word earns an additional five points.

After three or four clues, teams may run out of the letters they need. The game ends when teams can no longer play.

Say: **The only way to lose this game was to quit. As long as you kept playing until you ran out of letters, you won. The Christian life is like that; you can lose only if you quit.**

• **Describe a time you just wouldn't quit. What happened?**

• **What kinds of things discourage you when you want to follow God?**

TEAM FRISBEE
Proverbs 5:21-23
Sin

This game forces partners to work together while they play Frisbee. For every four children, you'll need a Frisbee.

Have two sets of partners play Frisbee. But the partners' arms must be linked at all times, or the partners' legs must be tied together with bandannas or ties.

Say: **When there's sin in our lives, it binds us.**

• **How would being free and unbound have changed your ability to throw and catch?**

• **Sin binds us. In what ways would lying bind someone?**

• **In what ways does sin bind you?**

GOOD NEWS COMIN'!
Isaiah 52:7
Evangelism

For this game, have children take off their shoes.

You'll need a beach ball.

Form a long line. Have children lie on their backs with their heads all pointing the same direction. Then—have kids using only hands and feet—pass the "good news" from one end of the line to the other.

When one player passes the good news, have him or her jump up and run to the end of the line to keep the good news moving. Play until you run out of room or until everyone has passed the good news several times.

Say: **We all like to get good news. And it's fun to give good news to others, too!**

• **What is some good news you've received by phone? by mail?**

• **Describe good news you were able to share with others.**

• **In what way is hearing about Jesus good news for you?**

GAMES WITH A MESSAGE

THE GRATEFUL LEPER

Luke 17:11-17

Healing

This game helps children experience having physical limitations.

For every two children, you'll need an elastic bandage, a glass of water, a

newspaper, and a buttoned jacket or sweater.

Form pairs. Have one partner from each pair wrap up the other's hands in elastic bandages so he or she can't use any fingers. Have the "handicapped" children complete the following exercises:

- drink a glass of water,
- page through a newspaper, and
- put on a buttoned jacket or sweater and button all the buttons.

Then switch roles so the other partner can experience the same.

Finally, do the same tasks without bandages.

Say: **Leprosy cripples those who have it. Imagine how happy a leper was when Jesus cured him!**

- **Describe a time you were sick or in pain and then you got better. How did you feel?**

- **In what ways would you like to see healing in you or your family?**

- **It's time we pray for God to heal our friends. Who do you want to pray for?**

BLIND TIMES
Mark 8:22-25
A blind man healed

This game helps children understand how it feels to be blind.

You'll need two blindfolds, a glass of water, paper, and pencils. Form two teams of equal size.

Have children from each team come forward to a table one at a time. Blindfold one child from each team. Then have teammates cheer as the two blindfolded children do these tasks:

- pour water into a glass,
- write their names on pieces of paper, and
- walk back to the team to tag the next teammate to come forward.

Say: **Jesus healed a blind man, restoring his sight.**

- **How did it feel to do the tasks in this game without being able to see?**

- **What do you think the blind man told his friends about Jesus?**

- **What will you tell your friends about Jesus this week?**

DODGING DRUGS

Romans 12:13-14

Drugs and alcohol

This game is a great warm-up activity for a meeting about drug abuse. You'll need a small ball of yarn (1 to 2 feet of yarn) for each child and some handkerchiefs for this game.

Form two teams. Give each child a ball of yarn. Tell children to try to hit someone on the other team with the ball of yarn on the count of three. Ask kids to pay attention to where they're hit with other balls of yarn. Then, on the count of three, let 'em at it!

After the balls of yarn have been thrown, have players each unroll the balls that hit them and loosely tie the yarn to the body part hit. If the head was hit, have children use the handkerchiefs to cover the closest feature (eyes, mouth, or ears). Not all players will be hit.

Children may not use the body parts marked with the yarn or handkerchiefs in any activity for the rest of the session. For example, those with arms marked can't write or catch, and those with blindfolds must depend on others to guide them.

After all other activities are completed, discuss how drugs are like the balls of yarn. They come at children from all directions, and unless children are determined to avoid them, they may give in. Then discuss how awkward it was to function while impaired and how drugs always impair people.

Say: **We can't be available to capably serve God if we're under the influence of drugs or alcohol. We're out of control.**

• **Describe a time you lost control of your body because of medication or an injury. How did it feel? How did it change your ability to do things?**

• **Why do you think God doesn't want us to get drunk?**

• **What have you decided to do about drugs and alcohol?**

DO-IT-YOURSELF STORYBOOKS

Ephesians 5:15-17

Time management

Use this activity to encourage creativity and teamwork. You'll need old magazines, a blank notebook, scissors, glue, and a pencil for each team.

Give your group members the opportunity to be instant artists, writers, and editors. Divide the group into teams of no more than four. Give each team a stack of magazines, a blank notebook, scissors, glue, and a pencil. Give each team fifteen minutes to find at least ten magazine pictures from which it can create a story. Ask children to glue each picture on a separate notebook page and write a line or two of a story under each picture. Stick with the fifteen-minute schedule. If children protest, remind them that artists, writers, and editors work under strict deadlines.

After the groups have finished their notebooks, get everyone together and have teams take turns reading their stories aloud.

Say: **It sometimes feels like we have all the time in the world, but that's not true. You have today to live only once.**

• **How did it feel to work under a deadline? When do you have deadlines?**

• **If you had time to do just the single most important thing today, what would you choose? Why?**

• **How well do you think you use your time? Why?**

DON'T GET RIPPED OFF!
Galatians 5:22-23
Joy

This is an interesting and fun way to look at things that can "steal" a person's joy. You'll need three beanbags each labeled "joy;" a blindfold; and name tags with words such as *worry, anger, jealousy, fear,* and *lack of sleep* written on them.

Ask for four volunteers. Blindfold one volunteer, and place the beanbags near his or her hand. Have the other three volunteers be "joy thieves" who'll try to steal the beanbags. Give each thief a name tag labeled "worry," "anger," "jealousy," "fear," "lack of sleep," or anything else that steals joy.

Each thief gets thirty seconds to steal a beanbag. As the first two thieves try, the blindfolded child may only stop the thieves if he or she hears them coming. He or she can't touch the beanbags. To stop the thief, the blindfolded child must listen carefully, then point and yell, "Stop thief!" The blindfolded child has three chances to point and yell at each of the first two thieves. For the third thief, allow the blindfolded child to rest one hand against the remaining beanbag(s). If the child feels a beanbag move, he or she may stop the thief.

Let children take turns playing the different roles.

Say: **Let's not let anything or anybody steal our joy!**

• **What things remind you of the joy you have in God?**

• **What things in life "steal" your joy?**

• **What makes you joyful today?**

SECRET AGENTS
Matthew 6:3-4
Serving others

This game teaches thoughtfulness through fun.

For each team you'll need construction paper, markers, a tape recorder and cassette, and transportation.

Before the meeting, decide what missions you'll have children accomplish. Possibilities include leaving cards on doorsteps of people the group appreciates, visiting someone who's sick, doing something for the church, or thanking a schoolteacher.

If the group is larger than six, divide into teams. Have each child choose a secret-agent name. Give each team a cassette recording that gives details of its mission. Each tape should say what the mission is, how long it'll take, and why it's an important mission. Have children leave a construction paper card or note, signed by each secret agent, at each mission site.

Encourage the secret agents to take a few minutes to plan their strategies before going out on the missions. Set a time for secret agents to meet back at the church and report on their missions.

Say: **We served others, and nobody knew it was us.**

• **How did it feel to be a "secret agent" of service?**

• **Describe a time someone helped you, but you didn't know who it was. What happened?**

• **In what way can you serve others today?**

TAKE A SEAT
Colossians 4:2
Thankfulness

This is a great way to discover what makes children thankful.

You'll need chairs, a CD or cassette player with music, tape, and squares of construction paper. Before the meeting, arrange chairs in a circle. Tape a square of construction paper under the seat of every second or third chair.

Have the group play Musical Chairs. Play a song, and have children walk around inside the circle of chairs. Then stop the music at random. When the music stops, have each child sit in a chair. Since there are enough chairs for everyone, no one will be "out." But when everyone is seated, have children check to see if there is a construction paper square under the seat of their chairs. Children sitting in chairs with construction paper squares must each share something they're thankful for.

Say: **We have lots to be thankful for. Let's talk about that.**

• **Describe the things that keep you from feeling thankful. How can you be thankful anyway?**

• **What makes you thankful today?**

TREASURE HUNT

Colossians 3:16

Gratitude

Here's an old favorite with a new twist.

You'll need twenty small pieces of construction paper. Before the meeting, write "treasure" words on the pieces of construction paper, such as the different fruits of the Spirit, family, friends, or the Bible. Hide the papers around the room or yard.

Form two teams. Allow four minutes for teams to comb the room or yard and find the hidden treasures. When time is up, have teams bring their treasures to you and read them aloud. The team with the most treasures wins.

For a variation on this game, make fifteen "true" treasures—such as family, friends, or the Bible—and five "false" treasures—such as money, candy, or toys. Then form two teams. Allow four minutes for teams to hunt for the treasures. When the time is up, have the teams separate true treasures from false treasures. Then have teams turn the true treasures in to you. Each true treasure turned in is worth two points, and each false treasure chosen as a true one takes away one point.

Say: **We often forget to express our gratitude to God.**

• **What are you grateful for that wasn't mentioned in our activity?**

• **If people got paid based on how much they express gratitude, how much do you think you would earn this week? Why?**

BiBLE-LEARNiNG GAMES

SPECiAL EFFECTS BiBLE CHARADES

Bible review

Add a twist to an old favorite by asking children to describe a Bible character using only sound effects so that other children can guess the identity of the Bible character. For instance, Noah might be identified when a child impersonates a thunderstorm followed by animal sounds.

Some characters to consider using include Noah, Judas, Jesus, Moses, Adam, Eve, Goliath, Elijah, and the Pharisees.

Consider letting children pick characters they wish to portray with sound effects. If nobody has guessed the character within sixty seconds, let children add motions to their descriptions. Still no correct guess? Then for the third sixty seconds, let children use words, too.

Say: **Imagine if someone had to guess who we were just from the sounds we make!**

• **What's a *sound* that sums up your life pretty well (if you like to play basketball, it may be the sound of a ball dribbling)?**

• **What's an *action* that sums up your life pretty well? What does it say about you?**

BIBLE-VERSE SCRAMBLE

2 Timothy 2:15
Memorizing Scripture

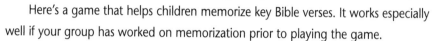

Here's a game that helps children memorize key Bible verses. It works especially well if your group has worked on memorization prior to playing the game.

You'll need 3X5 cards. Choose familiar Bible verses, such as Matthew 28:19. Then write one word of each Bible verse on a separate 3X5 card. For example:

Therefore	go	make	disciples
of	all	nations,	baptizing
them	in	the	name
of	the	Father	and
of	the	Son	and
of	the	Holy	Spirit.

Then make a duplicate of each set of cards. Mix up the cards in each set.

Form two teams. Give a set of face-down cards to each team. Have teams each form circles on opposite sides of the room.

On "go," have teams each throw the cards into the air. Then have children scramble to gather the cards. See which team can put the cards in correct order first. Then play again with another Bible verse.

Say: **Learning God's Word is important!**

• **How important—or unimportant—do you think it is to memorize God's Word?**

• **What do you think the benefits are of memorizing God's Word?**

• **How has knowing God's Word helped you?**

BOOKS OF THE BIBLE

Matthew 4:1-11

Memorizing Scripture

This quiet game helps children learn the order of books in the Bible. It works well in confined spaces.

Call several children to the front of the room. Name each one for a book of the Bible. For example, Chris is "Genesis," Beth is "Exodus," Matt is "Leviticus," and Gina is "Numbers." Have "books of the Bible" stand in the order they appear in the Bible and say their book names. Then have the rest of the group cover their eyes while the books of the Bible scramble. Have children open their eyes and put the books back in order. To make the game more difficult, choose books that aren't consecutive.

Say: **Jesus knew Scripture by heart and could quote it.**

• **How easy or hard is it for you to use the Bible?**

• **What would make it easier for you to use the Bible?**

• **Who can help you learn to use the Bible this week? What will you ask this person to do?**

FOUR GOSPELS

Psalm 119:9-11

God's Word

This is a great energizer for the middle of a preschool meeting.

Name each wall of the room for one of the four gospels. Then when you call out the name of a gospel, children turn to face that wall. When you call out, "Good news," children spin around. Vary the pacing.

There's no winning or losing, just play as long as you want.

Say: **Good job learning the names of the four Gospels! They're the first four books in the New Testament, and they tell us about Jesus.**

• **Why is it a good idea to know the names of the Gospels?**

• **Do you know anyone named after the Gospels—Matthew, Mark, Luke, or John?**

• **This week let's read one of the Gospels! Which one will you read?**

THE FRUITS OF THE SPIRIT

Galatians 5:22-23

Fruits of the Spirit

This fun activity can be done as a field trip or at the church.

You'll need apples, bananas, grapes, oranges, pineapples, strawberries, pears, peaches, watermelon slices, and small towels.

If you use the idea for a field trip, arrange for nine locations as "fruit stops." The locations can be homes, nursing homes, or institutional care centers. Have the group go to each stop and do an assigned "fruity" task. Instruct children to leave the fruit with the people at each stop. Or play the game during a group meeting.

The assignments:

• **Love**—Stand in a line and pass an apple while saying, "Jesus loves you."

• **Joy**—Use bananas for microphones and sing "I Have the Joy."

• **Peace**—Stand in a circle. Give each child some grapes, and tell everyone to pass the grapes to the person on the right at the same time while saying, "I'm passing peace to you, my friend."

• **Patience**—Stand in a line and pass an orange down the line under their chins. The person passing the orange says, "Patience works. It just takes time."

• **Kindness**—Each child gives a hug, and the group gives a pineapple to someone at the fruit stop or church. Together everyone says, "We're kind when we're giving."

• **Goodness**—Each child picks up ten pieces of trash and puts them in a trash bin. Give each child a strawberry to eat. Together say, "God is good, so let's eat something good."

• **Faithfulness**—Walk around in pairs. Have one partner close his or her eyes, carry a pear, and say, "I have faith you'll lead me in the right way."

• **Gentleness**—Using small towels as "baby blankets," cradle peaches in your arms like babies. Rock them gently while saying, "Gently, gently we rock you."

• **Self-control**—Stand in a line and pass a slice of watermelon without taking a bite. As the slice of watermelon passes by, have each child say, "I have self-control. I will not eat the watermelon."

When you've finished, read aloud Galatians 5:22-23. Then share watermelon with all of the kids and the people at your fruit stop or church.

Say: **The fruits of the Spirit are character traits that God wants to build into our lives through his Holy Spirit.**

• **Which of the "fruits" we handled seem most like you?**

• **Which of the "fruits" we handled seem least like you so far? (Remember, God isn't finished with you yet!)**

GOLIATH CAN'T CATCH ME
1 Samuel 17:1-54
Goliath

Choose one person to be "Goliath." Have that person stand in the middle of the room. Explain that Goliath can't move his or her feet but can bend over to tag children.

Other players tease Goliath by saying, "Goliath can't catch me," and seeing how close they can get without getting tagged. Each child who's tagged joins Goliath and also tries to tag others without moving his or her feet.

Continue playing until everyone has been tagged.

Say: **God showed his power when David defeated the huge warrior Goliath.**

- **How do you think the soldiers watching David and Goliath felt?**
- **In what ways have you seen God show his power?**

LISTEN CLOSE!
John 10:15-17
Hearing God

This game will remind children that they need to listen closely for God's voice!

Designate one person as the "shepherd." Ask another five or six children to be "false shepherds." Everyone else will be "sheep."

Place the sheep in the center of an open, empty room, and tell them to close their eyes. Ask the shepherd and false shepherds to then silently position themselves around the perimeter of the room and to all say, "Come here, sheep. Come to me." Instruct the sheep to say, "Baaaaa!" as they attempt to determine which way to go and to make their way toward the true shepherd. Sheep must keep their eyes shut the entire time.

After playing once, select a new shepherd and false shepherds. Play again, but this time the sheep won't make noise; they'll just listen and move. Again, the sheep must keep their eyes shut.

Say: **It's a challenge to find the true shepherd when there are lots of distractions around us!**

- **How did you feel when you were trying to find the true shepherd the first time? Why?**
- **Was it easier to find the true shepherd when you were talking and listening or when you were just listening? How is this like following Jesus?**
- **What or who does God use to speak to you?**

THE NOAH'S ARK SHOW
Genesis 6:9-22
Noah

Have kids each find a partner. Then have each pair secretly choose an animal from Noah's ark to act out for other teams to guess.

Have one pair go in front of the group and act like its animal, while other pairs try to guess the animal.

When a pair guesses correctly, it goes in front of the group and does its act. If that pair has already done its act, have the two kids choose another pair. This continues until all pairs have been in front of the group. The pair that guesses the most animals correctly wins.

Say: **Noah had a challenging job!**

• **Describe a challenging job you've had.**

• **What's something you think God wants you to do?**

THE PRODIGAL SON
Luke 15:11-32
The Prodigal Son

You'll need a balloon for each child. Write events from the parable of the prodigal son (Luke 15:11-32) on small slips of paper, one for each balloon. For example:

• Dad divides the property between his two sons.

• Younger son runs away with his money.

• Younger son spends his money.

• Younger son goes broke.

• Younger son decides to come home.

• Dad welcomes the son home.

• Older son gets mad at his dad.

• Dad throws a party because his younger son has come home.

Put one slip of paper into each balloon, and blow up the balloons.

Have children form a circle and bat the balloons around. When you yell, "stop and pop!" have children each grab a balloon, pop it, and retrieve the slip of paper.

Then have children together work out the correct sequence of the parable without looking at the Bible. Collect all bits of burst balloons.

When kids work out the correct sequence, read Luke 15:11-32 aloud.

Say: **Jesus told this story to help us understand God's love.**

• **What does this story tell you about God's love for you?**

• **Which character in this story reminds you of yourself? Why?**

SCRIPTURE HUNT

Psalm 119:17-19

Books of the Bible

Use this game to help children burn off energy while also learning the books of the Bible.

Write the names of all the books in either the Old or New Testament on separate 3x5 cards. Place the cards face down throughout your room.

The challenge: Children will pick up the cards and tape them on a wall or white board *in order*. That is, if you've written the names of Old Testament books, kids have to find "Genesis" first, tape it up, and then find and tape up "Exodus," and so on.

Time the children to see how long it takes them. Place a copy of the correct order somewhere in the room so they can use it for reference if necessary.

Say: **Knowing the order of the books of the Bible helps us locate Scripture references easily. It's a handy skill!**

• What do you find most difficult about learning the order of the books of the Bible?

• How would memorizing the correct order help you?

INSTANT TRANSLATION

Psalm 119:33-35

Understanding God's Word

This is a game in which two groups of children "translate" words by providing synonyms for common words. For instance, you might yell out, "Sphere!" and a team might reply, "Ball!"

The goal is for children to restate, in their own words, words and phrases you provide.

Form two teams. Call out a word to the first team, and give them three seconds to "translate" the word. If they can't, it goes to the second team. If neither team can suggest a word that works, it may tip you off that the children don't have a complete understanding of the concept represented by the word.

Alternate which team is chosen first.

Some words to use: sphere (ball), currency (money), Scripture (Bible), antibiotic (medicine), applause (clapping), custodian (janitor), tidings (greetings), rabbi (teacher), sea (ocean), and repentance (ask forgiveness). Use a thesaurus to find plenty more words! And add appropriate church and Bible concepts such as Pharisee, salvation, grace, fellowship, disciple, saint, and resurrection to see if children truly understand them.

Say: **Knowing words doesn't help much if we don't understand what they mean.**

• **What's something in the Bible you wish you understood better?**

• **What's something in the Bible you understand well enough to explain it to others?**

NAME THAT APOSTLE

Matthew 10:2-4

Learn the names of the twelve apostles

Use this matching game to help your students learn the names of Jesus' twelve apostles.

Before your meeting, create enough sets of cards so every trio of children can have one. To create a set of cards, write a different apostle's name on each of twelve 3x5 cards.

To play, have children form trios, and ask trios to pair up so three kids are facing three other kids. Have each trio place a set of cards face down on the floor without looking at what's written on any of the cards. Place the cards so each trio's cards form a rectangle, four rows of three cards.

Each trio will be a team. Ask each pair of teams to determine which team is wearing the most blue. That's the team in each pair of teams that will go first.

The first team will point out one of the other team's cards and ask the partner team to turn over that card and show what's written on it. Then the card will be turned face down again. Then the second team will do the same. Teams will continue taking turns until a team thinks it can match a pair of apostle names. That team will give it a try. If the attempt is successful, that team gets a point, and the cards are removed from play.

This is a memory game, so good remembering to you!

Say: **Remembering twelve names is hard, but knowing about the apostles is important.**

• **What's something you know about one of the apostles that surprised you when you learned it?**

• **In what way is one of the apostles an example to you?**

VOLLEY BALLOON REVIEW

Psalm 105:7-9

Review Bible books

Use this game to help children review the books of the Old and New Testaments. You'll need a few balloons.

Have children form a circle. Tell them they can move around during the game to help each other.

Inflate one balloon, and toss it to one child. Have that child tap the balloon into the air and say, "Genesis," the first book of the Old Testament. Before the balloon hits the ground, another child must tap it and say, "Exodus," the second book of the Old Testament. Continue the game until the books of the Old Testament are named in the correct order. The object of the game is to keep a balloon airborne throughout the entire listing of the Old Testament. Then do the New Testament books.

For variety, use other topics with this game, such as the disciples' names, the fruits of the Spirit, and the words of Scripture verses such as John 3:16.

Say: **God has a great memory, but ours isn't so good. That's why we have to review things we've learned—so we remember them!**

• **What's your earliest memory?**

• **How easy or hard is it for you to recall what God says in Scripture? Why?**

• **What's a Bible verse or truth that you never want to forget?**

STEP-BY-STEP QUESTIONS

Hebrews 12:1-2
Review of Bible characters

Use this game to review the lives of Bible characters you've introduced to your kids.

Form your children into two groups, and place them against opposite walls if you have a fairly small room. The children need to be about ten paces apart.

Give each team the name of a Bible personality you've studied. The other team will be able to ask up to fourteen yes-or-no questions to identify who the personality is. If the question is answered "no," the team with the answer will take a step toward the team asking the question. If the answer is "yes," the team with the answer will stand in place.

The goal is for the team that is guessing to come up with the answer before the team with the answer can touch them.

Say: **There are thousands of people we can meet in the Bible. We could play this game all day!**

- **Who's a Bible character who has had an influence on your life?**
- **Who's a Bible character you would like to know more about?**

ENERGY
BURNERS

ADAM AND
THE ANIMALS

Genesis 2:4-22

Adam

Choose one child to be "Adam." Have him or her stand at one end of the room. (See diagram below.) Have the rest of the group stand together behind a masking-tape line at the other end of the room.

Have Adam call out the name of an animal from the list provided. The children will try to move to where Adam stands and then return to the starting line, but they have to move like the animal mentioned.

Some animals to call include kangaroo, snake, sloth, elephant, worm, frog, and

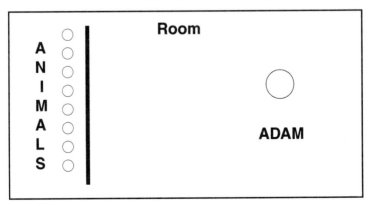

cheetah. Add animals to keep things interesting!

Say: **Adam was able to be with all the animals in a peaceful garden. What fun!**

• **If you could have any animals safely as a pet, what would you choose?**

• **Tell about the first pet you remember your family having. What was it?**

• **God gave Adam the job of naming the animals. What's a job God has given you?**

Barley Field

Proverbs 4:20-27

Guard your heart

A version of this game was played by children in the fields of Israel after harvest many years ago.

Play this game in a long, narrow area such as a driveway, sidewalk, or hallway. Select an area where it won't hurt to fall. Or mark an outside area with chalk dust. Divide the area into three sections. The center section is the barley field.

Two players are "It." They link arms and guard the barley field. Other players find partners and link arms. Each pair chooses one of the end sections as home base.

On a given signal, such as a whistle blow, players from the two end sections leave home base, enter the barley field, kneel, then return to home base. The guards of the barley field try to tag pairs in the field. Each pair tagged is frozen and must remain where tagged. The game leader watches the game and repeats the signal to enter the barley field as needed. The game ends when only one pair remains untagged. The winning pair becomes "It," and the game starts over.

Say: **It's hard to guard our barley field! And it's just as hard to guard our hearts from bad influences.**

• **What's something people see and hear that they shouldn't let themselves see or hear?**

• **If you could take any television show off the air, what show would you cancel? Why?**

• **What's something you've seen that you wish you hadn't seen?**

BLIND SHOE-SEARCH
2 Corinthians 4:17-18
Trusting God

This "sole" game helps children loosen up and have fun.

You'll need a blindfold for each child. Have children form a circle. Then ask them to take off their shoes and toss them in the middle. Mix up the shoes.

Blindfold each player. Then mix up the shoes again. On "go," have children try to figure out which shoes are theirs. Encourage them to try on different shoes. When children think they've found their own shoes, have them put on both shoes.

Play until everyone is wearing a pair of shoes. Then have children take off their blindfolds to see who has matching shoes and who doesn't!

Say: **We have a hard time trusting what we can't see and knowing something is true if we can't see it ourselves!**

• What was hardest about finding your own shoes in the stack? How could you trust what you couldn't see?

• What's something or someone you trust, even though you can't see it with your own eyes?

• Why do you think God is—or isn't—trustworthy?

AFTER-YOU SHOE BALL
Psalm 25:9
Humility

Ask children to each take off one shoe. Have children slip their right (or left) hands into their shoes so that the soles of the shoes are facing up. Have children form pairs, and ask children in each pair to sit on the floor, facing each other.

Give each pair a pingpong ball. The goal of the game is for each pair to bat the ball back and forth, keeping it in the air as long as possible.

A rule: After each "hit," the child hitting the ball must say, "After you," before his or her partner can hit the ball. Speak quickly!

Say: **To play this game you have to be humble by meeting your partner's needs (placing the ball where it's easy for your partner to hit) and by inviting your partner to play first.**

- **In what ways is it more fun to play games with someone who's humble?**
- **What is it about being humble that makes it possible for God to teach you his ways?**
- **When is a time you often find it hard to act humble? Why?**

Bus

Ecclesiastes 1:13-14
Chasing after things

This highly active game is a blast to play.

Line up chairs like seats in a bus. (See diagram below.) You'll need enough chairs for the number of people in the group, minus two. Choose one child to be the "chaser" and another to be the "chasee." Have the chaser and chasee stand on either side of the chairs. Have the rest of the children sit in the bus seats. As children sit down, have them introduce themselves and ask their fellow passengers, "If you could visit anywhere in the world, where would you go, and why?"

The chaser and chasee begin running around the outside perimeter of the seats. The chaser tries to tag the chasee. The chasee, however, can slide into any seat by pushing the child in that seat into the next seat. The person forced out of that seat then becomes the chasee. The chaser then pursues the new chasee. If the chaser tags the chasee, the roles reverse.

After the game has progressed for a while, yell, "I smell smoke!" Then have children change seats in a "fruit-basket-upset" manner. Make sure everyone moves, so the chaser and chasee can get seats and rest. The last two children left standing become

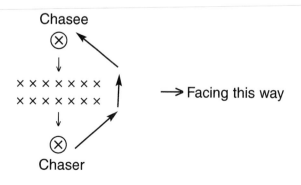

Chasee

Chaser

→ Facing this way

the new chaser and chasee. Flip a coin to see which becomes the chaser or the chasee, and start the game again.

Say: **There's no way to win this game. No matter how long we chase after the chasee, we *never finish*. Chasing after things is like that.**

• **How much money would you need before you had absolutely all you think you'll ever need in your whole life?**

• **When is a time you really, really, *really* wanted something only to find out when you got it that it wasn't all that great?**

• **What's something you really want right now, and why do you think it will—or won't—be a good thing to have?**

CHICKEN

Matthew 6:33-34
Focus

Chicken is a Hopscotch-type game played in China.

Have players each remove one shoe. Place the shoes in a straight line about one foot apart.

The first player hops on his or her shoed foot over each of the shoes in the line. When the player gets to the last shoe, he or she kicks that shoe out of line, then turns and hops back over the remaining shoes. If the player puts both feet on the ground at any time, a second player takes over at that place. The game continues in the same manner until all the shoes are kicked out of place. When all the shoes are kicked out of place, line them up again so everyone gets a turn.

Say: **It was hard to keep your balance during this game! The only way was to focus hard.**

• **What's something you do in life that takes all your concentration and focus?**

• **If you concentrate hard on obeying Jesus, how does that change your actions?**

CIRCLE TAG

1 Peter 5:8
The devil

Here's an active game that requires cooperation.

You'll need one bandanna. Choose one child to be "It." Have the rest of the group form a circle holding hands. Stick the bandanna in the hip pocket of one of the players.

"It" runs around the outside of the circle trying to grab the bandanna while the circle turns either clockwise or counterclockwise trying to save the bandanna. If the bandanna is caught, "It" joins the circle and a new "It" is chosen.

If you have a large group, try the game with two bandannas on two different players.

Say: **The Bible says the devil is like a hungry lion trying to catch us.**

• How did working together help protect us from having our bandanna "devoured"?

• What's one way the devil tempts you? How can other Christians help you?

DODGE BALL

Colossians 1:21-23
Evangelism

This game helps a restless group burn off excess energy.

You'll need a large supply of old newspapers and a garbage bag.

The object of the game is to wad up sections of newspaper and hit someone with them. Any child who's hit switches sides and becomes a thrower. There are no teams in this game; you'll play until everyone is a thrower.

Play the game in a room or gym. To begin, have everyone stand on one side of a line you created with masking tape on the floor about ten feet from a wall. Newsprint wads don't travel far, so you have to work in a contained area.

Start with one or two kids as "throwers" on one side of the line and everyone else up against the wall. Place the newspapers on the throwers' side of the line. As children are hit, they become throwers, scooping up paper wads and carrying them to the throwers' side of the line.

Say: **Once we were God's enemies because of our sin. Now we're his friends, and we can invite others to join us!**

• **In this game, everyone ended up on the winning team. How is that like inviting our friends to know Jesus?**

• **Who is someone you would like to tell about Jesus?**

GRAB-BASE TAG
Matthew 6:26-28
Worry

Select two children to play Tag. Have the child whose birthday is closest to today's date be the "chaser" and the child whose birthday is next closest to today be the "chasee." Have the other children form pairs and hold hands. If you have an uneven number of children, have an adult play. Have the pairs scatter over the playing area. They're the "bases."

The bases don't move as the chaser tries to tag the chasee, but they hold out their free hands, waiting to be grabbed. To get "on base" and avoid being tagged, the chasee grabs a free hand of one of the bases. Then the person at the other end of the pair becomes the chasee and runs away from the chaser. When the chaser tags the chasee, the chasee becomes the new chaser. The old chaser is allowed to grab a base, and another child is the new chasee.

If your group is large enough and you want to make the chase more challenging, reduce the number of bases. To do this, stop the game every few minutes and form bases of three, then four, then five people. As the bases get larger, one can be a different size than the others.

Say: **This is a game that can cause us to worry. Will we be chased? Where will we go if we are chased? It's easy to worry!**

- **Why do you think Jesus wants us to not worry?**
- **What's something that causes you to worry?**
- **What can you do to help you not worry so much?**

TAG TOE

Mark 10:13-16
Jesus and children

Use this game to set up a discussion about the disciples' reluctance to let children "interrupt" Jesus.

Choose one child to be "Jesus" and six children to be disciples. The rest of your children will play the part of...children!

Instruct Jesus to walk from one point in the room to another point that's about twenty feet away. Jesus must move by putting the heel of one foot to the toe of the other foot. The disciples will surround Jesus and attempt to keep children from touching Jesus.

An important detail: Everyone must keep his or her hands at his or her sides. No using hands to reach Jesus or keep people away from Jesus!

Say: **Jesus made time for children as well as grown-ups. And he has time for you!**

- **Why do you think Jesus liked to be with children?**
- **Why do you like to be with Jesus?**

MUMMY ME!

John 11:1-44

Lazarus

Have children form trios, and give each trio a roll of toilet paper and a garbage bag.

The goal of the game: Each trio will have four minutes to turn one child in the trio into a mummy. The first step is for each trio to determine who'll be the mummy and who'll be the mummy-makers. Then get them started with a "Ready, set, go!"

As children work, give updates on how much time is left to work.

When time has elapsed, have children step back and applaud each other's handiwork. Then have all the "mummies" burst forth and emerge from the wrapping. Ask trios to then clean up all the toilet paper.

Say: **If we had *really* been wrapped in linen cloths, like Lazarus was, it wouldn't be easy to get out. We would need help...lots of help!**

• **What's the biggest help Jesus provided Lazarus?**

• **If you were standing outside Lazarus' tomb when Jesus raised Lazarus from the dead, what would you have said? Why?**

• **What does Lazarus being raised from the dead mean to you?**

HEART-TO-HEART TREASURE HUNT

Luke 12:33-34
Possessions

For this game, you'll need one heart-shaped cookie for each child and twenty heart-shaped pieces of paper.

Before children arrive, hide nineteen of the pieces of paper around your meeting room. Put some where they're easily seen and others in less obvious places, such as under the seats of chairs, in a book, or elsewhere in your room. Tape one very small heart on the bottom of your shoe.

Tell children you have a treasure for them to claim—one cookie each. But you won't give them their treasure until they've found and returned all twenty hearts to you. Add some energy by announcing a time limit.

If children don't ask to see the bottoms of your shoes, don't volunteer to show them. But eventually help children find all twenty hearts, and share the treasure!

Say: **You were willing to do a lot of work to claim your treasure. I could tell your hearts were in it!**

• **What's something you've saved for and bought yourself?**

• **What's something you once thought was amazingly cool and now you don't care much about anymore? What changed?**

• **Luke 12:33-34 says we can have treasure in heaven. Why is it better for you to have treasure in heaven than on earth?**

SHOWDOWN

1 Samuel 17
David and Goliath

Form your children into two teams, and have them stand shoulder to shoulder along two opposing walls facing each other. Designate one team to be "David" and the other team to be "Goliath."

Explain that this game is a reminder of how David and Goliath walked toward each other across an open plain. In real life, David won. In this game, it can go either way!

Ask teams to walk slowly toward each other. At some point, as they approach each other, you'll say either "David" or "Goliath." If you say, "David," members of the David team will attempt to *gently* tag a member of the Goliath team as the Goliath team turns and runs back to its wall. Once a Goliath team member is touching the wall, that person is safe. All tagged Goliath people join the David team. If you say, "Goliath," *that* team does the chasing. Don't use a predictable pattern as you call out teams to do the chasing.

Say: **This game got your hearts racing because you didn't know whether you would be chasing someone or being chased.**

• **How do you think Goliath felt as he walked toward David? Why?**

• **How do you think David felt as he walked toward Goliath? Why?**

• **How do you feel when you face a big challenge? Where do you go for help?**

GROUP FUN

ANiMAL FLASHCARDS
Genesis 7:1-5
Noah

Children need to be quick to play this game!

For each player, you'll need a set of ten animal cards. All sets must be identical. These can be made by gluing animal pictures or printing animal names on 3x5 cards.

Form players into pairs. Each player will shuffle his or her own set of cards and lay them face down on a table. Then both players in a pair will turn up the top cards of their decks at the same time. If the cards match, the first player to call out the name of the animal on the cards collects both cards. If the cards don't match, players will try again. When they have gone through all the cards in their decks, the players shuffle the cards they collected and start again. The goal is to match up as many cards as possible in three minutes.

Say: **Imagine how hard it was for Noah to match up animals so that he had two of some animals and seven of others! He must have been busy!**

• **What do you think is the most amazing part of Noah's life? Why?**

• **If you had been asked to vote one kind of animal off the ark, what would you have left behind? Why?**

• **What's one way in which you would like to be like Noah? Why?**

MIRROR, MIRROR
1 Corinthians 11:1-2
Modeling

Play this game to help children see how their actions impact others.

Have children form pairs and stand facing each other. Ask the person in each pair whose birthday is closest to Christmas to go first.

The goal of the game is for children in pairs to mirror each other's actions *exactly*.

Ask the first child to act out the following story in such a way that his or her partner can "mirror" each action. Create other stories (or review Bible stories) to let children take turns leading or mirroring actions.

There once was an explorer who went to the pyramids. First she packed her backpack. Then she put on her backpack. Then she locked her house. She walked from her house all the way to the ocean. She walked uphill, and she walked downhill. She walked in the wind. She walked in the rain. When she came to the ocean, she jumped in and started to swim. She did the crawl. She did the backstroke. She finally reached the shore of Egypt, where she shook herself off and climbed onto a camel. The camel carried her across the desert. She was hot. She went up and down as the camel walked. And finally she reached the pyramids. She was so tired that she fell over!

Say: **You did a great job influencing your partners. They followed your every move!**

• **Is it a good thing or bad thing if someone mirrors your life? Why?**

• **Describe someone you've tried to "mirror" in life. Who was it? Why did you want to be like that person?**

DINOSAUR-EGG HUNT
Galatians 5:22-23
Fruits of the Spirit

This fun game turns fruit into "dinosaur eggs" for a scavenger hunt.

You'll need various kinds of fruit that might pass for dinosaur eggs, such as watermelons, cantaloupes, grapefruits, and oranges.

Before the group arrives, hide the dinosaur eggs. When the group arrives, explain that dinosaurs have been seen in the area and the group has been asked to look for the eggs. Tell children it's very important that they find the eggs before they hatch, or there'll be a dinosaur population explosion. Describe the eggs' colors, sizes, and shapes.

Send the children to look for the eggs. Have them bring the eggs back to a central location. After one egg is found, the idea will catch on.

After all of the eggs are found, have two helpers clean them and prepare them to be snacks.

Say: **Good hunting! Of course, these aren't really eggs—they're fruit. And there's another kind of fruit you should know about.**

 • **What's a fruit of the Spirit you see in someone else in our class?**
 • **Which of the fruits of the Spirit do you see in yourself?**

ELASTIC CIRCLE
Matthew 5:22-24
Friendship

This activity provides a good stretch in the middle of a meeting.

Have children hold hands in a circle and pretend to form an elastic band. Have the circle stretch out as far as possible, then go inward, then stretch out again until the circle breaks. Then have children form small elastic bands of two or three.

Say: **Sometimes we have arguments that cause us to "stretch" in our friendships. We have to forgive each other, share with each other, and listen to each other.**

 • **What's something that causes you to "stretch" in your friendships?**
 • **What's something that you've done that caused your friends to stretch?**
 • **What could you do today to make yourself a better friend?**

FRACTURED MATCHES
2 Corinthians 6:14-15
Relationships

Form two teams. Give each child a piece of paper and a marker. Designate one team to be the "Adjectives" and the other team to be the "Nouns."

Have children each write one word on their pieces of paper from their teams' categories. For example, Adjective team members might write "striped," "pink," or "ugly." Children on the Noun team might write "zebra," "car," or "movie star."

Have the Nouns form a circle and hold their pieces of paper so everyone can read what they wrote. Have the Adjectives form a circle inside the Noun circle and also hold up what they wrote.

Play music. Have the Nouns walk clockwise and the Adjectives walk counterclockwise. When the music stops, have each Adjective child pair up with the Noun person closest to him or her. Then have each pair read its words together—for example, "striped car," "pink zebra," or "ugly movie star." Then play the music again, and have the circles move until the music stops. Play several times to hear many different crazy combinations.

Say: **When you don't have anything in common with your partner, you get some odd combinations!**

• **Who's someone with whom you have a lot in common? What do you share?**

• **Why do you think it's a good idea for a Christian to marry someone who shares his or her faith?**

• **Can you describe a character trait of the person you're going to marry (think ahead!)?**

FUN FOR THE FRUGAL
Matthew 6:32-34
Good stewardship

Check out these games that children love. They're easy to set up and inexpensive. They can be used for vacation Bible school, camps, or fellowship meetings.

• **Ring the Prize**—Pound a nail in the middle of a block of wood so the nail head sticks up. Cut out the centers of plastic coffee-can covers. Have children toss them over the nails for prizes.

• **Candy Game**—Buy lots of suckers. Color the tips of the sticks on about one-fifth of them. Poke holes in a box top, and stand the suckers up with the tips inside the holes so they aren't showing. Have each child select a sucker. Award prizes to children who choose suckers with colored tips.

• **Bowling**—Set up a "bowling alley" using toy bowling pins and a softball. Use a table with boards along the sides so the softball won't roll away. If children roll a strike, they'll receive a first prize. If they roll a spare, they'll get a second prize.

• **Fish**—Place a tall sheet of plywood against a table. Make fishing poles from long sticks and string, using paper clips as hooks. Have children drop their lines over the plywood, and have someone hook prizes on them.

• **Football Through the Tire**—Hang some old tires from sturdy tree limbs. Have children throw footballs through the tires for prizes.

• **Ball in the Basket**—Have children throw a ball into a clothes basket. Or challenge children to toss the ball through a hoop and into the basket.

• **Boat Game**—With waterproof markers, mark numbers on the bottoms of some inexpensive toy boats. Place the boats in a pan of water. Have each child select a boat. The number on the boat they pull out indicates what prize they win.

• **Feed the Cartoon Character**—Paint a cartoon character on a sheet of plywood. Cut out the mouth. Have children throw a ball or a beanbag into its mouth for a prize.

Most novelty stores have small prizes for a few cents each. Or bulk prizes can be ordered through novelty companies. Distributors often have coloring books, storybooks, and puzzles they'll donate.

Say: **We didn't spend a lot of money on this game, but we had lots of fun playing it.**

• **What's something you like to do that doesn't cost any money?**

• **Why do you think God wants us to be responsible in how we use money?**

• **When it comes to using money wisely, what do you find difficult?**

GUESS WHAT'S GROSS
Proverbs 14:12
Making wise choices

This activity always gets lots of laughs as children get "in touch" with some items that feel gross but which they might enjoy eating.

You'll need whatever items you can think of that feel gross. See the list for a few ideas.

Ask for five volunteers to be on a panel. Have the volunteers sit in front of the group at a table. Blindfold them. Then have each child feel the items one at a time using touch only. The child who guesses the most items correctly wins.

Some examples:

• wet pickles,

• ketchup,

• olives,

• applesauce,

• relish,

• cooked chicken livers, or

• cooked spaghetti.

Say: **Some of you thought the items felt gross, but they're items you frequently eat!**

• Describe a time you thought an activity or food would be gross but you liked it. What was it?

• What's a yucky job you've done because it helped someone else?

• What's a yucky job you could do this week to serve someone?

GREEN LIGHT GO!
Romans 2:12-14
Obedience

This game gets a group together.

You'll need three blankets, towels, or sheets—one red, one yellow, and one green. Lay the blankets side by side on the ground. Tell kids the colors represent a traffic light.

Have all the children stand on the yellow (middle) blanket. When you shout another color, have the children quickly move to the appropriate blanket. The last child to get both feet on the correct blanket is eliminated from the game.

To make the game more challenging, occasionally call out the color on which the children are already standing. Anyone who steps off that blanket is eliminated.

For a change of pace, call out "traffic accident" and have everyone vacate all blankets. The last child to get off is eliminated.

Keep the pace quick, and vary the colors called. The winner is the last person to remain in the traffic light.

Say: **We often don't like to obey rules, especially other people's rules!**
- **What's a rule you have to obey as a child? Why?**
- **What's one of God's rules you want to obey? Why?**
- **What's a rule you don't like to obey that you'll obey this week?**

"I" GAME
Romans 12:10
Care for others

This activity helps children focus on others rather than themselves. You'll need ten dried beans for each child.

As children arrive, give them each ten beans. Have children mingle and talk about their previous week. Whenever someone says, "I," any listener who catches it gets a bean. Count beans after five minutes.

Say: **It's hard to not talk about ourselves!**
- **Who is someone who listens to you and helps you feel special?**
- **Why do you think God wants us to care about others?**
- **Who is a friend you care about?**

IN THE BIG FISH'S MOUTH

Jonah 1:1-17
Jonah

Have preschoolers count off by threes. Have all the Ones become "big fish" and spread throughout the room, moving their arms like fish's mouths.

Have the Twos each find a big fish and stand inside its mouth, so each One is hugging a Two.

Then have the Threes "swim" around the room, mimicking a swimming stroke and waiting for an empty fish's mouth to stand in.

When you yell, "Switch," all Twos leave the big fish's mouths and compete with the Threes to quickly swim inside another big fish's mouth. Continue playing the game by yelling, "Switch!"

Say: **Being swallowed by a big fish would be scary! Jonah must have been frightened.**

* **What's something that's scary to you?**
* **What helps you feel better when you're scared?**

MOUSIE

1 Peter 5:7-9
Sin

Games similar to this were played in the Victorian era. It plays best in a room with lots of furniture.

Choose one child to be the "mother mouse" and another to be the "owl." Other players are "baby mice."

The mother mouse leads the baby mice, crawling under chairs and around tables. The babies must follow her route exactly. When all the babies are following the mother, signal the owl to start. The owl also follows the path of the mother exactly, trying to catch the babies. If the owl can crawl fast enough, he or she can catch the last baby in line. Any time after the owl starts, the mother mouse can stand and run back to the starting place. The baby mice stand and follow her and the owl chases them. When the owl catches a baby, either crawling or running, the captured baby becomes the owl and the owl becomes the mother mouse for the next game.

Say: **Good job catching the mice, you owls! But did you know there's someone chasing you right now, too? It's the devil, and he wants you to do something wrong and sin.**

• **How does it feel knowing that the devil wants you to sin and disappoint God?**

• **God tells us that if we sin and we ask to be forgiven, he'll forgive us. How does that make you feel?**

• **Let's pray now and ask God to forgive us. Will you join in that prayer?**

MUSICAL HUGS

John 13:34-35
Loving others

Count how many preschoolers are present. If you have an odd number, great. If you have an even number, ask an adult volunteer to join the game.

Have children jog around the room to music. When the music stops, have each child hug the person closest to him or her. The person left out will choose one other person to sit out with him or her. Then start the game again. Play until one child is left.

Have the last child stand in the middle of the group for a big group hug!

Say: **Giving and getting hugs is fun!**

• **Who is someone at your house who you like to hug?**

• **How does it feel when someone you love gives you a hug?**

• **Who do you know who needs a hug? When will you hug that person this week?**

NUMBER HUGS

Hebrews 10:24-25
The Church

Choose one person to be "It." Have the rest of the children spread out around the room. Then have "It" call out numbers between two and the number of children playing.

As soon as the number is called, have children run and form a group hug with that many people. For example, if "three" is called, have groups of three children hug together. Of those left out from each hug, choose one person to be "It."

Say: **Here's the good news: You'll never be left out when you're adopted into God's family!**

• **When is a time you felt left out at a church activity? What happened? How did you feel?**

• **What can you do to make sure nobody else feels like you did?**

Y'ALL COME
Galatians 3:26-28
The Church

Before playing this variation of Tag, mark out a specific playing area. You'll need to allow room for children to move about and have a reasonable opportunity for escape.

Designate one child to be "It." That child will dash about until tagging someone. Then the two will join hands and run *together* to catch a third person, who'll also join the growing "It" organism.

Play until every child has joined the winning team.

Say: **No matter who you were when you were tagged, you joined the winning team and helped out. You couldn't lose!**

• **How did it feel to join the winning team? Why?**

• **In what ways are Christians all alike? unique?**

• **In what ways are you unique and special?**

SHOWERBALL
Ecclesiastes 4:9-10
Teamwork

This game combines the best of basketball and water balloons and is played outside.

You'll need to prepare some water balloons.

Line up the group from tallest to shortest, and count off by fours. Ones and fours make one team, and twos and threes make the other team. Explain that the game is played and scored just like basketball. But because water balloons are used instead of a ball, certain modifications to the rules are necessary:

• The balloon can't be dribbled. It must be passed from player to player. No player may run with the balloon.

- If a balloon breaks in play, a new one is put into play by the opposing team.

- To count as a score, the balloon must pass through the hoop before it breaks.

- Intentional or rough physical contact between players is a foul, and the balloon goes to the other team. There are no foul shots.

- If the boys tend to leave the girls out of the game, a rule can be added that requires boys to pass the balloon to girls and girls to pass the balloon to boys.

The game ends at a preset time or score or when the supply of balloons is exhausted.

Have kids clean up the mess at the end of the game.

Say: **We did better at this game when we worked as a team. Life's like that!**

- **What's something in life that requires teamwork?**

- **What do you like best about being on a team? What do you like least?**

- **What makes it easy for you to be on a team? What makes it difficult? What can you do to make it easier to be on a team?**

SOUND-EFFECTS GAME

Genesis 1
Creation

Form teams of no more than four. One at a time, give teams a sound to make. Players can use only their voices and their bodies (slapping knees, clapping, stomping feet) to produce the given sounds. Here are some "sound" ideas:

- fans of a losing football team,
- chickens at feeding time,
- preschoolers at a fast-food restaurant,
- a stock-car race,
- the percussion section of a marching band,
- thoroughbred horses in a race,
- a passenger train at full speed,
- tap dancers in a chorus line,
- popcorn popping, or
- a clock shop at noon.

Say: **You know, the Creation must have been noisy at times! Think about everything God created, then answer these questions:**

• **What do you think is the noisiest thing God created? How did it sound?**

• **What's a favorite sound from your own life? How does it remind you of God's creation?**

SOUP'S ON
1 Corinthians 12:11-13
Talents and skills

This game later becomes a meal at a retreat or other event.

You'll need masking tape, a large soup pot, a ladle, water, a can opener, cups, spoons, and access to a stove. Ask children to each bring a can of their favorite condensed soup to the meeting. Have a couple of extra cans available for anyone who forgets.

On a tile or smooth concrete floor, put a strip of masking tape for the starting line. Eight feet from that strip, put another strip of masking tape about four feet long.

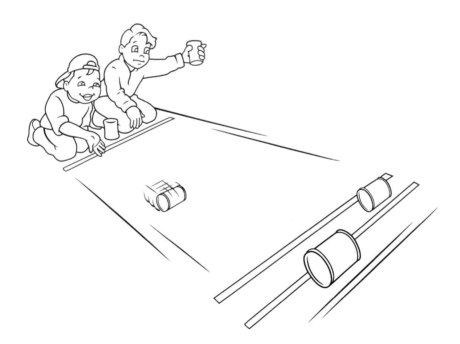

Five inches beyond that strip, put another four-foot strip. Put a fourth four-foot strip another five inches away.

Have the children stand behind the starting line and take turns rolling their cans of soup. Cans that stop between the second and third strips are worth ten points. Cans that stop between the third and fourth strips are worth twenty points. Cans that pass the fourth strip are worth five points. The scoring is collective; everyone rolls, and all the points are added into one score. If a can stops in the first ten-point spot, children can try to nudge it into the twenty-point spot with another can to improve the score.

When children are tired of playing, have them open their cans and put all the soup in the pot with equal amounts of water. Heat it to boiling, and serve this one-of-a-kind soup for your meal.

Say: **We all contributed to making our unique soup, and it wouldn't taste the same if we hadn't all helped.**

- **In what ways can you contribute to your family?**
- **In what ways can you contribute to church and our class?**

WATCH OUT DOWN UNDER
Luke 21:19
Faithfulness

Choose one person to be "It." Have the rest of the group form a circle around "It." Have children in the circle stand with their feet spread a shoulder's width apart, touching the next player's feet.

Then have "It" stand in the center of the circle with a ball. Have him or her try to roll the ball out of the circle between someone's legs. The ball can't leave the ground, and players can only use their hands to stop the ball. They can't move their feet. When someone lets the ball out of the circle between his or her legs, he or she becomes the next "It."

Say: **To succeed in this game, you had to stand firm!**

- **What's a time it was hard for you to stand firm in your Christian faith?**
- **When do you find it easier to stand firm in your Christian faith?**
- **What would help you stand firm in the future?**

ZOO LOVE
Genesis 1
Adam and Eve

Children love to go on field trips to the zoo. Here's an idea for helping them learn what animals love.

You'll need a list of questions and a pencil for each team.

Take the group to your local zoo, and divide into teams of no more than four, plus one adult. Give each team a list of zoo-love questions. Ask teams to meet at a designated spot and time.

The zoo-love questions:

• Which animal would you love to hold?

• Which animal would you love to kiss?

• Which animal loves to climb trees?

• Which animal loves the beach?

• Which animal would you love to hug?

• Which animal loves the forest?

• Which animal loves to run?

• Which animal loves to be cold?

• Which animal loves dirt?

• Which animal loves the sky?

• Which animal loves mountains?

• Which animal loves water?

• Which animal loves to sleep?

• Which youth leader loves to eat?

Say: **Even if you don't love all animals, you can usually find one you like! Imagine how much fun Adam and Eve had!**

• **What's the first pet you or your family had? What do you remember about the pet?**

• **If you could have any animal for a pet, what would you pick? Why?**

• **When you think about your favorite animal, what does that animal reveal about God's power and creativity?**

RELAYS

BAREFOOT RELAY
Psalm 119:133
Relying on God

For this goofy variation of the common relay, you'll need a few marbles. Form equal teams. Have kids take off their shoes and socks. Designate a goal about twenty feet away.

Have each team form a single line. Give the first player of each team a marble to put between his or her toes. On "go," have each child hobble to the goal and back without losing control of the marble and with his or her eyes closed. Teammates will call out directions. If the child loses control of the marble, he or she must run back to the starting line and begin again.

When a child successfully hobbles to the designated point and back without losing control of the marble, he or she tags the next child and gives that child the marble.

Say: **There was no way to do this without listening to your teammates!**

• **What was the benefit of listening to your teammates?**

• **How has listening to God changed your life?**

• **How will you listen to God this week?**

COTTON-BALL RELAY
Exodus 16:10-20
Manna

This easy, indoor relay race involves two or more teams.

For each team, you'll need a spoon, a piece of construction paper or poster board, a goal marked on the floor, and a large bowl filled with cotton balls.

Give the first child on each team a spoon and piece of construction paper or poster board. The race begins as the first player on each team uses the spoon to gather a cotton ball from the bowl. He or she holds the spoon with the cotton ball in it in one hand and the paper in the other hand. The player carries the cotton ball in the spoon across the room and drops it on the goal on the floor. Then using the paper as a fan, the player fans the cotton ball along as he or she walks back to the team. Then the child hands the spoon and the paper to the next player and the relay continues.

A variation is to have a leader stand near the goals and call out different things for the players to do while carrying or fanning the cotton ball, such as hop on one foot, walk backward, crawl, skip or walk sideways.

Say: **It was hard to gather cotton balls, but God made it easy for the Israelites to gather manna and be fed in the desert.**

 • **How do you think the Israelites felt the first time they saw manna?**
 • **What's a good gift God has given you?**
 • **How can you thank God for the good gifts he has given to you?**

DADDY-LONG-LEGS RELAY
Proverbs 18:24
Friendship

This energy releaser requires kids to work together.

You'll need a two-foot length of rope for each person.

This is a long version of the traditional three-legged race. Form equal teams of four to seven people. Each team stands side by side behind a designated starting line. Hand each child a length of rope. Have each child tie his or her right ankle to the left ankle of the person on his or her right. All teammates should be tied to each other.

Have each team coordinate which ankle pairs should step forward first. When all teams are ready, have them race to a goal and back.

If your group has less than eight children, form one daddy-long-legs team and race the clock. Run several races and see if faster times can be achieved.

Say: **In this relay, we had to care about our partners because we couldn't leave our partners behind.**

• **In what ways is this like being in the church?**

• **Who's a friend who has stuck with you during a difficult time?**

• **How can you become a friend who sticks with others during hard times?**

JOYFUL POPPIN' RELAY
Acts 3:1-8
Joy

For sheer enjoyment of racing and popcorn, try this one.

You'll need a paper plate for each person, popcorn, and three buckets.

Form two teams. Have team members line up. Put a bucket of popcorn at the

center of a designated goal line and an empty bucket at the head of each team line. Give each child a paper plate. On "go," have the first relay runner on each team hop to the goal, grab a handful of popcorn, put it on the paper plate, and hop back. Have him or her empty the popcorn into the team bucket. Give each team member a turn. The team with the most popcorn at the end of the game gets to be first in line when you serve fresh popcorn for a snack!

Say: **Imagine not being able to walk. Now imagine being healed instantly in the name of Jesus. You would be hopping with joy!**

• **What's something Jesus has done in your life that has brought you joy?**

• **If you could use just three words to describe what Jesus has done to bring joy into your life, what would they be?**

• **Who will you tell your three words to this week?**

BROTHER, MAY I? ICE-CREAM-SUNDAE RELAY

Romans 14:14-16
Respecting others

For every four children, you'll need a pint of ice cream, chocolate syrup, toppings, and spoons.

Form teams of four players each. Give the first person in each team one pint of ice cream and a spoon. Give the second person in each team chocolate syrup. Give the third person some toppings. The fourth person will eat.

On "go," the first person scoops some ice cream and gives the spoon to the second person who adds chocolate syrup to it. Then the second person gives the spoon to the third person, who feeds the fourth person, but only after the fourth person asks, "Brother, may I?" If the third person objects, the ice cream won't be eaten.

After the fourth person swallows the ice cream, he or she runs to the start of the line, grabs a new spoon, scoops ice cream from the pint, and starts it down the line again as all the team members shift one position.

Say: **You got the ice cream, but only if eating it didn't create a problem for the person feeding you. Maybe if I was on a diet, I would find it hard to watch you eat ice cream, or if I were diabetic.**

• **How did it feel to need someone's permission to enjoy your ice cream?**

• **When is a time you saw someone put another person's feelings and concerns above his or her own? What happened?**

• **When is a time you helped someone by putting yourself last? Who could you help that way this week?**

MASTERPIECE RELAY

Nehemiah 1:1–5:19

Teamwork

This relay helps build teamwork skills and is also just plain fun.

You'll need crayons, masking tape, and large pieces of paper.

Form teams of no more than five, and give each team a set of crayons. A short distance from the teams, tape large pieces of paper to a table or wall. You may want to put newspaper on the wall around each paper. On each large piece of paper, write a caption describing a picture to draw. Each team should have the same description. Make the description complex enough so each team member will have at least one item to draw—for example: (1) A man in blue jeans (2) sits in a sailboat (3) drinking cola (4) while reading a book (5) on a choppy ocean.

In relay style, have one team member race to the canvas, draw one of the descriptions, and check off what he or she has drawn. Have that child run back and tag the next person, who continues the picture. The first team to successfully complete its masterpiece wins.

Other masterpiece ideas include:

• (1) On the green chalkboard (2) the teacher with gray hair (3) and the student wearing orange and blue ribbons (4) did math problems.

• (1) The baby in the cradle (2) who held a bottle of grape juice in one hand (3) and a red-striped rattle in the other (4) wore a pink and blue baby bonnet (5) and was crying as loudly as she could.

Say: **Great job! When you first started, your pictures didn't look much like masterpieces in the making. You all had to do your part before the pictures took form.**

• **What do Nehemiah's experiences teach you about teamwork?**

- **What's a project in which you did your part and it helped?**
- **How can you do your part at home this week?**

PAPER-CUP RELAY
Mark 10:27
Power of God

Are your children all wet? They will be after this wild relay!

You'll need a paper cup for each child.

Form two teams. Have each team stand in a straight line. Give each team member a small paper cup to hold with his or her teeth. Fill the first child's cup on each team with water. Have each player pour water from his or her cup into the next person's cup using his or her teeth. No hands are allowed.

The team with the most water in the last person's cup wins.

Say: **All things are possible with God, but not with us. Sometimes we need help!**

- **What would have helped you do a better job of moving water?**
- **Describe a time you got help from God. What happened?**
- **How would you like God's help this week?**

PEANUT-SCOOP RELAY
Proverbs 14:29
Patience

Here's a fun relay that can be done either indoors or outdoors.

You'll need plenty of packing peanuts, a bowl, and two jars of equal size.

Form two equal teams. About twenty feet away, set two jars of equal size with the lids off. Have team members stand in a straight line. Place a bowl of packing peanuts next to the first person on each team.

On "go," have the first person on each team scoop up as many peanuts as he or she can hold with only one hand. Players must keep their other hands behind their backs with their palms open.

One at a time, have players run to their jar and dump in the peanuts. They can't pick up any dropped peanuts. Then have the players run back and tag the next teammate, who does the same. When all children have taken a turn, count the peanuts in each jar.

Say: **Sometimes when we rush, it actually slows us down because we make mistakes.**

- **How did being patient help in this game?**
- **When do you find it hard to be patient with others or yourself?**
- **How can you be more patient at home this week?**

SPELLING-BLOCKS RELAY

Matthew 7:14

Discernment

Here's another fun idea for a relay event.

You'll need a set of alphabet blocks for each team. Borrow them from your church nursery, or purchase them from a local toy or discount store.

Form equal teams. Line up teams behind a starting line. Place a pile of alphabet blocks for each team on the floor at the opposite end of the room. Give teams a word to spell with the blocks. Make sure beforehand that each pile of blocks has all the letters needed for the particular word or phrase you want children to spell, and that teams have words of equal length. On "go," the first child on each team runs to the team's pile of blocks and finds the first letter of the word the team must spell. He or she runs that block back to the team. The second teammate runs to the block pile and finds the second letter. The first team to spell the word then cheers for the other team. Then have children return all the blocks to their respective piles and move on to a new word.

Say: **When you ran to pick up a block, you had lots of choices, but only one choice was right. Life is like that sometimes!**

- **When is a time you had to make a difficult choice?**
- **What help does God give you in making right choices?**
- **What's a difficult choice you have to make for which you need God's guidance?**

SURPRISE-STUNT RELAY

Philippians 4:13
Relying on God

This relay will keep children on their toes because they won't know what they need to do next. The materials you'll need will depend on the activities you choose.

Form teams of equal size. Fill one paper bag for each team with plastic bags that include written instructions and materials for each team member to do a stunt. Some ideas:

• Eat a cracker. Then whistle a verse of "Amazing Grace."

• Tie a yarn ankle bracelet around a teammate's ankle.

• Blow up a balloon. Tie it. Then sit on it and pop it.

• On a teammate's cheek, use lipstick to draw a heart and color it in.

• Place a peanut between your knees, and hop back to your team without losing the peanut.

Place the paper bags, with plastic bags inside, about twenty feet away from the teams. On "go," have the first child from each team run to the paper bag, pull out one plastic bag, perform the stunt, and run back to tag the second child in line.

Have teams play twice, attempting to improve their times.

Say: **You had to do some hard things to play this game! Sometimes God asks us to do hard things, but he helps us!**

• **Which activity that you did seemed hardest when you were about to do it?**

• **What's something difficult that God has helped you do?**

SCRIPTURE INDEX

TOPICAL INDEX

ENERGY-LEVEL INDEX

KEY

High Energy—involves running or walking; active physical interaction of children.
Moderate Energy—involves use of large-muscle groups but little or no movement.
Low Energy—fun, but little movement.
    You can also tweak most games to turn up—or down—the energy level. And be mindful that when children and adults jump in and start playing, almost any game becomes higher energy! Have fun!

HIGH ENERGY GAMES

MODERATE ENERGY GAMES

LOW ENERGY GAMES